Uncharted, Unexplored, and Unexplained

Scientific Advancements of the 19th Century

Charles Babbage
and the Story of the First Computer

Mitchell Lane
PUBLISHERS

P.O. Box 196
Hockessin, Delaware
19707

Uncharted, Unexplored, and Unexplained

Scientific Advancements of the 19th Century

Titles in the Series

Alexander Graham Bell and the Story of the Telephone
Antoine Lavoisier: Father of Modern Chemistry
Auguste and Louis Luminiere and the Rise of Motion Pictures
Charles Babbage and the Story of the First Computer
Charles Darwin and the Origin of the Species
Dmitri Mendeleyev and the Periodic Table
Florence Nightingale and the Advancement of Nursing
Friedrich Miescher and the Story of Nucleic Acid
George Eastman and the Story of Photographic Film
Gregor Mendel and the Discovery of the Gene
Guglielmo Marconi and the Story of Radio Waves
Henry Bessemer: Making Steel from Iron
Henry Cavendish and the Discovery of Hydrogen
J. J. Thomson and the Discovery of Electrons
James Watt and the Steam Engine
John Dalton and the Atomic Theory
Joseph Lister and the Story of Antiseptics
Joseph Priestley and the Discovery of Oxygen
Karl Benz and the Single Cylinder Engine
Louis Daguerre and the Story of the Daguerreotype
Louis Pasteur: Fighter Against Contagious Disease
Michael Faraday and the Discovery of Electromagnetism
Pierre and Marie Curie and the Discovery of Radium
Robert Koch and the Study of Anthrax
Samuel Morse and the Story of the Electric Telegraph
Thomas Edison: Great Inventor

Visit us on the web: www.mitchelllane.com
Comments? email us: mitchelllane@mitchelllane.com

Uncharted, Unexplored, and Unexplained

Scientific Advancements of the 19th Century

Charles Babbage

and the Story of the First Computer

Josepha Sherman

Uncharted, Unexplored, and Unexplained

Scientific Advancements of the 19th Century

Copyright © 2006 by Mitchell Lane Publishers, Inc. All rights reserved. No part of this book may be reproduced without written permission from the publisher. Printed and bound in the United States of America.

Printing   1   2   3   4   5   6   7   8
Library of Congress Cataloging-in-Publication Data
    Charles Babbage / by Josepha Sherman.
        p. cm. — (Uncharted, unexplored, & unexplained)
    Includes bibliographical references and index.
    ISBN 1-58415-372-5 (library bound)
    1. Babbage, Charles, 1791–1871—Juvenile literature. 2. Mathematicians—Great Britain—Biography—Juvenile literature. I. Title. II. Series.
QA29.B2S48 2005
510'.92—dc22

2004024613

ABOUT THE AUTHOR: Josepha Sherman is a prolific author with more than 60 books in print. The owner of Sherman Editorial Services, Josepha has also written a six book series on alternative energy (Capstone); *The History of the Internet* (Franklin Watts); *Bill Gates: Computer King* (Millbrook); and *Henry Cavendish and the Discovery of Hydrogen* and *J. J. Thomson and the Discovery of Electrons* (both for Mitchell Lane Publishers). In addition, she is a native New Yorker, has a degree in archaeology, loves to tinker with computers, and follows the NY Mets.

PHOTO CREDITS: Cover—Time Life Pictures/Mansell/Getty Images; p. 6—Charles Babbage Institute; pp. 8, 36, 38—New York Public Library; pp. 10, 22, 30, 33, 39, 40, 41—Science Museum; p. 12—Library of Congress; p. 18—Graeme Robertson/Getty Images; pp. 19, 20, 34—Science and Society.

PUBLISHER'S NOTE: This story is based on the author's extensive research, which she believes to be accurate. Documentation of such research is contained on page 47.

The internet sites referenced herein were active as of the publication date. Due to the fleeting nature of some web sites, we cannot guarantee they will all be active when you are reading this book.

Uncharted, Unexplored, and Unexplained

Scientific Advancements of the 19th Century

Charles Babbage

and the Story of the First Computer

Chapter 1   An Idea Is Born 7
                 FYInfo*: The Abacus 11

Chapter 2   A Mathematician's Boyhood 13
                 FYInfo: The Napoleonic Wars 21

Chapter 3   The Difference Engine 23
                 FYInfo: John Herschel 29

Chapter 4   The Analytical Engine 31
                 FYInfo: Ada, Countess of Lovelace,
                       Mathematician 35

Chapter 5   A Bitter End 37
                 FYInfo: The Great Music War 42

*For Your Information

Chronology 43
Timeline of Discovery 44
Chapter Notes 45
Glossary 46
Further Reading 47
Works Consulted 47
Index 48

This formal portrait of Charles was painted in his later years. It shows a man who had become rather bitter about life.

1

An Idea Is Born

One warm summer night in 1815, John Herschel, a young English astronomer and mathematician, called on his equally young mathematician friend, Charles Babbage, in Charles's home in London. The two men had been friends since their boyhood school days. They still really enjoyed being in each other's company, particularly when there were science problems for the two of them to unravel together. They both were full of curiosity about how things worked.

John had brought this night's problems to Charles in two big files of paper, each containing page after page of calculations. These seemingly endless lists of numbers were mathematical tables. The two friends had agreed to go over the tables before they submitted them to the Royal Society, England's foremost association of scientists.

Computers had made up the lists—but these were not the computers of the modern age. In 1815, there were no such things as machines called computers. There was no Internet or television. There weren't even electric lights. Those 1815 computers were people whose job it was to compute, or do mathematical calculations, by hand—which was then the only way that anyone could do math.

John Herschel was Charles's good friend. He was also a top astronomer. Here, though, there isn't a hint of the scientist. He is portrayed as an Englishman of good style.

When John and Charles separated the files into two piles, they had two different sets of figures, worked out by two different groups of human computers. Side by side, the men went down the lists, comparing the two, hoping that both lists would agree, proving the calculations correct.

Wait. There was an error in one list.

Wait, again. There was an error in the other list.

And there was still another error in the first list.

The two friends looked at each other in frustration. With all those errors, the tables could not be used. They would have to be recalculated by hand and checked yet again in the same tedious fashion—and even then there was no guarantee that the figures would be correct. Human beings were just too likely to make mistakes, especially when they had to deal with such long and complicated lists of numbers. In fact, in 1834, a survey of 40 books of numerical tables found 3,700 errors—and those were only the mistakes that had been found.[1]

It got even more complicated. There were three different places that errors could be made. The first were those made by the people adding up the figures. The second were those made when their addition was copied into a form that could be printed. The third were typographical errors, mistakes made by the printer.

It was all too much for Charles to take. Suddenly he shouted, "I wish to God these calculations had been executed by steam!"

By that, he meant done by a steam-powered machine that wasn't going to make human errors. Such a thing didn't exist—not yet.

At that thought, the two men stared at each other, both of them realizing what Charles had just unexpectedly proposed. There already were mechanical devices such as the French invention, the Jacquard loom, that used punched cards to automatically guide the loom's weaving. Why couldn't Charles, who loved tinkering with machinery, design a machine to do calculations and other work?

"It is quite possible," John said.

Charles was already plotting out how such a machine might work. It was quite possible, indeed, he thought. He got so excited over the idea that he actually made himself sick and had to force himself to relax. Yes, he would work on this project, but there was no rush. He would do the work carefully and logically. After all, he'd been a sickly child. Charles certainly didn't want to make himself a sickly adult as well.

But he was going to build that machine. He knew it.[2]

The Jacquard loom was designed in 1801 by French-man Joseph-Marie Jacquard. Its purpose was to make weaving simpler. It used punched cards, cards with special holes punched in them, to guide the loom's weaving.

There is an ancient ancestor to the computer, although it has to be operated by hand and isn't electronic or automatic. This instrument is called the abacus. An abacus is made up of a frame that holds columns of beads strung on wire or sometimes on thin strips of wood. A crossbar divides the frame into two parts, upper and lower.

Nobody knows for certain who first invented the abacus or where it was first used. Earlier, simpler versions seem to have existed thousands of years ago as counting stones or boards—flat surfaces with lines on them to hold counting stones—but no one can trace their origin, either. While the ancient Greeks, ancient Romans, and medieval scholars, among others, all used slightly different versions, the Chinese abacus, which is called the suanpan, or counting board, is the one most commonly used today.

In this Chinese version of the abacus, the first column of beads on the right is the ones column. The next column to the left of that is the tens column. The third column represents the hundreds, and so on down the rows to the left.

The beads in the ones column represent numbers one to nine. Each bead below the crossbar has a value of one, and each bead above the crossbar has a value of five ones, or five. In the tens column, the beads represent numbers ten to ninety. Each bead below the crossbar represents one ten, and each upper bead represents five tens, or fifty. By moving the right beads to or from the crossbar, an abacus user can add or subtract. A skilled abacus user can perform calculations as quickly and accurately as someone using a pocket calculator.

Trinity College is part of Cambridge University in Cambridge, England. It looks much the same today, at least from the outside, as it did when Charles attended. Inside, though, it is as modern as any other major university.

2

A Mathematician's Boyhood

December 25, 1791, must have been a very nervous Christmas day and night for Benjamin and Elizabeth "Betsy" Babbage. The couple had been married for only a little more than a year, and Mrs. Babbage was about to give birth to their first child.

Benjamin Babbage wasn't a young man; he was somewhere in his thirties at this time. A very practical fellow, he had waited to find a wife until he knew he could offer his bride a stable life. Mr. Babbage, a good, solid, respectable banker, had a house in London and another in the nearby town of Walworth. The land in Walworth had been in the family for hundreds of years. It was close enough to where Mr. Babbage worked in London for him to walk to work, yet far enough out of the city, he thought, so that a family could be raised, if need be, in the healthier air of the countryside.

Now, waiting for his first child to be born, Mr. Babbage must have been a worried man. How long would his poor wife be in labor? Would the baby be a boy or a girl? Above all, would it be healthy? In the late eighteenth century and through the first half of the nineteenth century, many English children died at birth or before they were a year old.

The baby, a boy, finally did arrive, though he missed being a Christmas baby by one day. Born on December 26, 1791, he was named Charles by his happy parents. Record keeping at the time wasn't always accurate, and the year of birth is also listed as 1792, just as the place of birth isn't always given.

What is known is that Charles grew up in London, which at the time wasn't as crowded as it would become a few decades later. Most of the people of England still lived in the country, on farms or in small villages. The terrible fogs of pollution that would come to blanket London and which would be caused by the burning of soft coal were still in the future. Even so, the air wouldn't have been too clean, thanks to carelessly tossed garbage, horses in the streets, and poor sewers; and there were already traffic jams caused by horse-drawn carriages and wagons.

Charles survived his first year, and his parents began to hope that he would live and grow strong. He showed intelligence at an early age and was always curious about how things worked. In fact, he often took toys apart, not to break them, but to study how they were made. Charles also seems to have been a brave and sensible little boy. When he got lost at age five, he didn't get scared the way most children would have done, but kept quite calm. Remembering, as he says, "[to watch] the passing vehicles . . . to find a safe opportunity to cross [a] busy street," Charles found his way to a shopkeeper he knew, who sent word to his family to come and get him.[1]

From about age five until he was eight, for all his calm courage, Charles was not a healthy boy. He suffered from one illness after another. His parents grew frightened for him. Two boys had been born after Charles, and both had died before their first birthdays. Mr. and Mrs. Babbage didn't want to lose Charles, too.

The Babbages decided that the wisest thing to do was to send Charles away from London, out into the cleaner countryside. They found a small school for him in the town of Alphington, in Devonshire. The program there offered to teach the boy English, Latin, Greek, and mathematics. That was considered to be quite a good education.

Charles did all right with the language programs, but he fell in love with mathematics then and there. At eight years old, he already had a good grounding in basic arithmetic—simple adding, subtracting, multiplying, and dividing—but he became fascinated with more complicated calculations and logic puzzles.

He applied logic to many situations outside of school. He wanted to know the truth behind stories. At age ten, Charles terrified a friend with stories about people who had called up the devil. Charles wasn't afraid. He was already aware that a good scientist had to test his theories, so he actually did try to summon the devil to see if any of the stories were accurate. As he says, he didn't actually want anything from the devil. "I simply wanted an interview . . . simply to convince [myself] of his existence."

No devil appeared, and Charles was satisfied—although he admitted that he prayed a great deal after that, just in case. But then he reasoned that "an almighty and all-merciful God" would not punish a boy who had used scientific experiment to test a theory. From that day on, Charles had no problem believing in both science and religion, and he kept that equal belief all his life.[2]

By the time he was about eleven, Charles had recovered his health, to his parents' great relief, and they moved him to a school in Enfield. Today Enfield is a London suburb, but back then it was a separate town. The most wonderful thing to Charles about that new school wasn't the classes. It was the school library, which held over three hundred books on all types of subjects. Charles learned a great deal from reading there, and he remembered that library with pleasure all his life, noting, "I think it of great importance that a library should exist in every school-room."[3]

It was in that library that Charles taught himself the advanced form of mathematics known as algebra. Because this was beyond the range of his regular lessons, he began secretly studying there from three to about five in the morning with two other boys who shared his passion for learning. This secret studying went on until other boys heard about the adventure and joined the group. Of course, once so many boys got

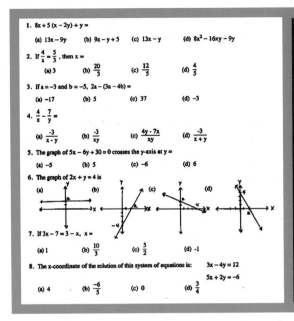

1. $8x + 5(x - 2y) + y =$

   (a) $13x - 9y$ (b) $9x - y + 5$ (c) $13x - y$ (d) $8x^2 - 16xy - 9y$

2. If $\frac{4}{x} = \frac{5}{3}$, then $x =$

   (a) 3 (b) $\frac{20}{3}$ (c) $\frac{12}{5}$ (d) $\frac{4}{3}$

3. If $a = -3$ and $b = -5$, $2a - (3a - 4b) =$

   (a) -17 (b) 5 (c) 37 (d) -3

4. $\frac{4}{x} - \frac{7}{y} =$

   (a) $\frac{-3}{x-y}$ (b) $\frac{-3}{xy}$ (c) $\frac{4y-7x}{xy}$ (d) $\frac{-3}{x+y}$

5. The graph of $5x - 6y + 30 = 0$ crosses the y-axis at $y =$

   (a) -5 (b) 5 (c) -6 (d) 6

6. The graph of $2x + y = 4$ is

   (a)   (b)   (c)   (d)

7. If $3x - 7 = 3 - x$, $x =$

   (a) 1 (b) $\frac{10}{3}$ (c) $\frac{5}{2}$ (d) -1

8. The x-coordinate of the solution of this system of equations is: $3x - 4y = 12$; $5x + 2y = -6$

   (a) 4 (b) $\frac{-6}{5}$ (c) 0 (d) $\frac{3}{4}$

Algebra is a branch of mathematics. In it, symbols, usually letters of the alphabet, represent numbers or members of a specific set of numbers. Charles would have studied and solved problems like these.

together, studying was quickly forgotten. On one special night the boys left the library, stormed the school playground, and set off fireworks. It must have been great fun, but of course they'd made too much noise to get away with their prank. The next morning, the school headmaster put a firm stop to any more early morning activities.

Charles's parents didn't seem to have known what to do about their bright and clever son's education. When he was in his early teens, they sent him to Cambridge to study with a clergyman. When the clergyman proved not to be a very good tutor, they moved their son to Totnes Grammar School. There the boy had a tutor from Oxford University; he was a strong teacher who made sure that Charles could read Greek and Latin. Those were the two scientific languages of that time, and Charles knew that he would need them in his studies. Charles continued, meanwhile, to teach himself further forms of mathematics.

Being a born scientist, full of curiosity about how things worked, Charles also tried out various experiments. One of these, after he'd read the New Testament account of Jesus walking on water, was an attempt to walk on water. He didn't use faith or magic, but science, with the help of a mechanical device he made out of two planks held together with hinges. He planned to use these as an early form of water skis, but the makeshift contraption collapsed in the middle of the first test, and he nearly drowned instead.

In 1810, at the age of eighteen, Charles passed the difficult entry exams for Trinity College, which is part of Cambridge University in Cambridge, England. Trinity College is a very old school. It was founded by King Henry VIII in 1546, though by Charles's time most of the original buildings had been replaced by newer ones. He entered the college in October 1810, being admitted mostly on the grounds of his proven self-taught mathematical skill. Charles eagerly looked forward to finally getting some formal education in higher mathematics.

He was soon to be disappointed. Although the university is one of the finest today, with a long list of successful graduates, the early nineteenth century was one of the lowest times in Cambridge University's history. It was a period when topics such as mathematics weren't being taught very well. Charles quickly realized that he had a better grasp on the subject than did any of the professors. At least, he told himself in consolation, he now had access to all the scientific papers of the great thinkers of England and the rest of Europe, so he reluctantly but gamely went back to teaching himself.

He did have some fun to go along with the studying. By this time, the sickly boy had grown into a healthy young man who was full of energy and laughter. Charles admitted that he'd been a little shy when he first entered the large world that was Cambridge University, with its hundreds of students. Since he was a friendly young man, he quickly overcame the shyness and soon came to like the people he found there.

Charles couldn't decide on just one club or special interest group, and he found himself part of the various academic and sailing clubs. He also joined clubs whose members studied the supernatural, such as the Ghost Club. He seems to have liked just about every school activity and to have made friends easily. Charles wrote, "My chief and choicest [group] consisted of some ten or a dozen friends who usually

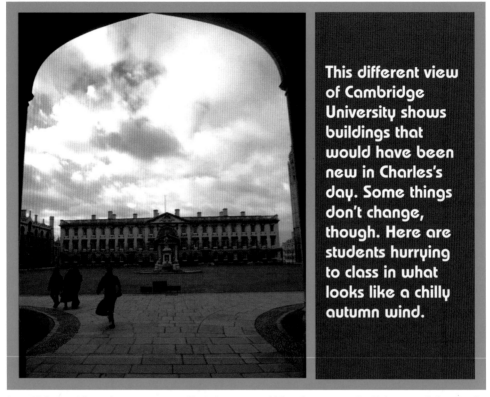

This different view of Cambridge University shows buildings that would have been new in Charles's day. Some things don't change, though. Here are students hurrying to class in what looks like a chilly autumn wind.

breakfasted with me every Sunday. . . . We discussed all knowable and many unknowable things."[4]

Since, like many other college students then and now, he received a strict allowance by his father, Charles kept careful and very honest accounting records. He even mentioned that he'd had some wine with friends at a party one night and—in the cold, snowy winter of January 1811—that he'd bought himself a pair of ice skates.

In 1811, at one of the many parties that the college students attended, Charles met a young lady, Georgiana Whitmore. A miniature portrait of her shows Georgiana to be a gentle, pretty, sweet-faced person. Portraits of Charles at that time show a strong-featured, good-looking man. The two young people liked each other's looks right away and began talking. Soon they found that they liked each other as people, too, and they started meeting more and more often.

Looking at this charming portrait of Georgiana, it's easy to see why Charles fell in love with her. She looks very pretty with her stylish tiara on her head. But she also has a sweet, gentle expression.

Meanwhile, Charles wasn't forgetting about his studies. He was still hungry to learn more about advanced mathematics. He tried to buy an important book on calculus by French mathematician Sylvestre Lacroix, but getting that book wasn't easy. At the time, England was at war with France, and most French items were not available in England. When Charles finally did find a copy of the text, he had to spend about seven pounds for it. That would be like spending about a hundred dollars on a book today.

Once he had the book, he had to translate it into English so that both he and other students could read it. This gave Charles an idea: Why not set up a society for such scientific translations? And so he began the Analytical Society, which was set up in 1812, with nine mathematicians attending, including Charles's friends and fellow students John Herschel and George Peacock. It was at about this time that Charles writes, "I was sitting in the rooms of the Analytical Society . . . in a kind of dreamy mood [over an open book of calculus]. . . . Another member . . . seeing me half asleep, called out, 'Well, Babbage, what are you dreaming about?' to which I replied, 'I am thinking that all these tables . . . might be calculated by machinery.'"[5]

However, he wasn't at the point yet of actually trying to design such a machine.

Here is Benjamin Babbage, Charles's father. He looks like the sort of man who rarely laughs. This picture may have been drawn at about the time he was so angry at his son for marrying Georgina.

All through 1812, Charles and Georgiana met and kept on meeting—we would say that they went on several dates—and they soon fell deeply in love. Charles told his father about the young lady he now knew that he wished to marry, and he was probably expecting to receive Benjamin Babbage's blessing.

Instead, to Charles's shock, Mr. Babbage was furious at his son. He had nothing against Georgiana Whitmore or her family, his father said, but marrying in such haste at such a young age was foolish. Didn't Charles know anything about his father's history? Hadn't *he* waited until he had a secure business position and steady money before even thinking about marrying? How dare his son do anything as risky as wanting to marry now, when he was not even a graduate. How did Charles expect to support a wife and family?

Charles didn't care what his father said or thought about it. He and Georgiana loved each other, and they did intend to marry, with or without Benjamin Babbage's blessing. Charles graduated from Cambridge in late spring of 1814, and shortly after that, on July 2, he and Georgiana Whitmore became husband and wife.

Charles Babbage grew up in a nation at war. In 1789, the French Revolution, a time of uprising against the king and the royal court, had brought about the downfall of the monarchy and the death of the royal family.

England protested the violence. The new French government ignored the protests and seized the neighboring country of Belgium. England opposed the invasion. In 1793, France declared war on England.

Napoleon Bonaparte

The series of connected battles that followed that declaration became known as the Napoleonic Wars. They were named after Napoleon Bonaparte, a soldier from the island of Corsica who had rapidly risen to power in France and who became its leader in 1799. Napoleon was a small man with a fierce nature. He wished to become the emperor of all Europe.

In 1803, Napoleon plotted to invade England. But in 1805, his battle fleet was stopped short by the English navy, led by the heroic Admiral Horatio Nelson. Napoleon was soundly defeated at the battle of Trafalgar, off the southwest coast of Spain.

That wasn't the end of the Napoleonic Wars. Napoleon controlled almost all of Europe. He commanded its countries not to allow any English goods into their markets. England promptly sent its navy to blockade, or block off, France from the rest of the world, letting no one in or out. England also helped Spain revolt against the French in 1808.

The last English battle with Napoleon was the battle of Waterloo in 1815, where he was finally defeated by the Duke of Wellington—who later became England's prime minister—and sent into lasting exile.

This is a working model of what Charles's Difference Engine would have looked like. Although he never finished his machine, he left many notes, charts, and diagrams. Later scientists were able to follow them.

3

The Difference Engine

Charles Babbage had graduated from Cambridge and was a married man—but he was suddenly without his father's help. Only a small yearly allowance that had been promised to Charles years before did Mr. Babbage grudgingly continue. Trained as a mathematician, Charles had to find something practical that he could do with his knowledge.

Between them, Charles and Georgiana had just enough money to keep them comfortable if they watched their expenses carefully—but that wasn't satisfactory for Charles. He was not the sort to sit idly. He did consider becoming a churchman, but that occupation, he admitted, didn't really fit him. Actually, his fascination with everything from algebra to lighthouses didn't really allow him to fit neatly into any category.

Not being able to focus on just one subject doesn't seem to have bothered Charles too much. Even with money worries, he was very happily married, and on August 6, 1815, he became a father for the first time, when Georgiana gave birth to a son. They named him Benjamin Herschel Babbage, the first name after Charles's father and the middle name after Charles's dearest friend John Herschel. Perhaps because of the hard feelings between Charles and his father, who still did not approve of his marriage, everyone always called the boy by his middle name, Herschel. Georgiana Babbage, not surprisingly, didn't care much for Charles's father, either.

Meanwhile, Charles was writing busily. In 1815, he presented no fewer than twelve papers on mathematical subjects to the members of the Royal Society of London. He also published several other papers on many different types of mathematics and logic.

The next year, on March 14, Charles was elected a member of the Royal Society. He wasn't very impressed with the society, though. About it he said, "The Council of the Royal Society is a collection of men who elect each other to office and then dine together at the expense of this society to praise each other over wine and give each other medals."[1]

Getting a paid position in something that suited him was beginning to seem almost impossible for Charles. At the same time, the need to do something was becoming more important. There was a second son now, named Charles after his father. (There would be eight children in all, although, as was the sad story with many families of the time, only three, Herschel among them, lived.) Charles really did need to find a way to make more money. In 1816, he applied for the job of professor of mathematics at Haileybury, part of the East India College in London. He was rejected because—it was hinted—he didn't have enough income. In 1819, a professorship of mathematics in Edinburgh, Scotland, became available. When Charles applied he was turned down again, this time, he was told in whispers, because he wasn't a Scotsman.

These frustrations didn't stop Charles and his wife from having fun. They were still very much in love. Whenever the growing family allowed it, Georgiana would travel with Charles to visit friends or see interesting things in England. Charles was a cheerful, high-spirited fellow in those days, and had a good sense of humor. A younger friend of his, H. Wilmot Buxton, who wrote a book of memories about him, describes Charles as someone who "always appeared cheerful and . . . retained the same outward show of gaiety to the world. He possessed an unlimited fund of humour," but "never . . . willingly gave pain" to anyone.[2]

Unlike many other scientists—who hid themselves away in their libraries or laboratories—Charles was a well-liked member of London society. He loved to tell funny stories and to laugh at the stories of others. He often went to parties, and he held his own parties on many Saturday nights. People loved to come to these. Sometimes, in fact, his parties attracted over two hundred people!

Unfortunately, there was a darker side to Charles's nature. He was very sensitive to insults—even when no insult was meant. He would brood on the comments and in his mind make them nastier than they were. This problem wasn't too bad when he was still a young man, but it would become worse as Charles grew older.

Charles shows his sense of humor in reporting an incident that happened when he and John Herschel went to France in 1819, after the war was over. They had stopped for breakfast and Charles, who spoke French, ordered two eggs for himself and two for John, *"pour chacun deux,"* which means, "two for each of us." The waiter misheard and thought that the two strange Englishmen had ordered *cinquante deux* eggs—which means fifty-two eggs! Charles stopped the waiter just in time from putting in that really overdone order.[3]

When Charles returned to England in 1819, he became interested in astronomical instruments, and he also began working out some details for what would become his difference engine. In fact, he started working on a small test model.

Meanwhile, no matter how Charles might have felt about the Royal Society, he continued to join other groups. In 1820 he was elected a fellow of another scientific organization, the Royal Society of Edinburgh. In the same year he helped to found the Royal Astronomical Society, and he served as its secretary for the first four years.

By 1822, Charles had finished his small model of a difference engine. He announced it to the Royal Astronomical Society on June 14, 1822, in a paper called "Note on the application of machinery to the computation of astronomical and mathematical tables." But Charles needed funding if he was to build a genuine, working difference engine. In July of that year, he wrote to the president of the Royal Society, describing what he wanted to make: "calculating machines . . . [that assist] the human mind in the operations of arithmetic. Some few of these perform the whole operation . . . once the given numbers have been put into the machine."[4]

It took a year after his request for money to be processed. On July 13, 1823, the Astronomical Society awarded Charles a gold medal for his development of the difference engine—but that didn't pay the bills. Charles reports on the government's lack of understanding of what he was doing. "On two occasions I have been asked [by members of Parliament], 'Pray, Mr. Babbage, if you put into the machine wrong figures, will the right answers come out?'"[5]

The Royal Society did try to help him. They sent a letter to the English government that said that Charles had "displayed great talent and ingenuity in the construction of his machine for computation," and that they considered Charles as "highly deserving of public encouragement, in the prosecution of his arduous undertaking."[6]

Charles also met with the Chancellor of the Exchequer, the government official who handled England's finances. The chancellor finally did grant Charles the money he needed and gave him the go-ahead to start work. Unfortunately, no one took notes of what actually took place at this meeting, so there are no recorded details about it. It is known that Charles started work in earnest in July 1823. The difference engine that he began building used the decimal number system—one to ten—and was powered by the user cranking a handle.

There was a huge obstacle—not in the design of the engine, but in the technology of Charles's time. The difference engine was going to need hundreds of perfectly made parts, possibly as many as 25,000. At the time, though, there was no way to make any of those pieces perfectly. There was also no way of automatically making more than one copy of a piece. According to Charles's design, the finished engine, if it was ever actually made, would stand about eight feet tall, seven feet wide, and three feet deep. There was no doubt about it. Building the difference engine wasn't going to be easy—or cheap.

In 1824, Charles made his first formal attempt at fund-raising. He took on a freelance job to create life expectancy tables for an insurance company. It must have taken too long and earned too little money, because he never tried that again.

Charles was always interested in more than one thing at a time. With his friend John Herschel, he performed some experiments on magnetism in 1825. Neither of them made any major discoveries.

At first 1827 looked as though it would be a good year for Charles. Work on the difference engine was coming along nicely, and he published a table of logarithms calculated with the aid of machinery. After the first few months, though, 1827 quickly became the most horrible year in Charles's life. In it, he lost the three people most dear to him: first his father; then his son Charles; and the last and heaviest blow of all, his beloved wife, Georgiana.

The strain of so much grief in so short a time was almost too much for Charles. He nearly had what is now known as a nervous breakdown, a complete mental collapse, and fled England. Charles wandered about Europe for over a year, visiting with other scientists and not even thinking about the difference engine.

While he was traveling through Europe, Charles's scientific curiosity gradually returned. In Germany, he studied a new invention, the stomach pump, and took one apart to see how it worked. He also jotted down notes about designing new improved carriages.

In Austria, he actually had a carriage built, following his design. It seems to have resembled a horse-drawn motor home, with a bed, a small cooking stove, a small dresser for his clothes, and various "pockets" for his books and tools.

In Italy, Charles was rather disappointed to have just missed one of the many earthquakes that took place near Naples. Instead, he studied

Mount Vesuvius, an active volcano that has erupted several times in human history. In A.D. 79, the most famous eruption—and the most violent one so far—buried the Roman towns of Pompeii and Herculaneum. Charles wasn't afraid of the volcano. He even climbed up to the summit, taking measurements of lava and steam. It was so hot up there that when he came back down again, he found that his heavy protective boots were falling to pieces.

It was also while he was in Rome, Italy, that Charles read a short newspaper item from Cambridge. It said, "Yesterday, the bells of St. Mary's rang on the election of Mr. Babbage as Lucasian Professor of Mathematics." This came as quite a surprise to Charles, as he hadn't even known he was being considered for the post. His first response was to refuse the honor, but once he was back in England, his friends told him that it would be wrong for him to disappoint the people who had voted for him and reject such praise. Charles reluctantly accepted.[6]

By the end of 1828, the Royal Society grant had been used up. The government didn't seem at all interested in giving Charles any more money. Charles had to finance the construction of his machinery himself—and that wasn't easy, since the difference engine required almost three tons of steel, brass, and pewter clockwork. In 1829, a group of Charles's friends asked for help from the prime minister, the Duke of Wellington. This was the same Duke of Wellington who had defeated Napoleon Bonaparte at Waterloo. Wellington actually did go to see a model of the difference engine. He was impressed enough to order another grant for the project and to hire an engineer to build it and make sure everything was done correctly.

As luck would have it, just then one of Charles's greatest personal problems surfaced: He was too interested in too many things to concentrate long enough on one project to get it completed. The difference engine wasn't more than half finished when Charles came up with the idea of another, more sophisticated machine. He called this an analytical engine.

John Herschel was both an astronomer and a mathematician —in fact, Charles claimed that his friend was better at mathematics than he. John became an astronomer in a case of "like father, like son": His father was William Herschel, the astronomer who discovered the planet Uranus.

Like Charles, John had many interests. He even tried his hand at earning a legal degree, but he quickly realized he wasn't going to be a lawyer. In 1816 he finally decided to follow his father's lead into astronomy.

John didn't waste the research he'd already done on other subjects, though. In 1819, he published his chemical and photography experiments, which proved to be very useful in the development of photography. In 1821, the Royal Society awarded him the Copley Medal, their highest award, for his work in mathematics.

Charles and John traveled together often. They went to Italy and Switzerland in 1821, sharing their love of mountain climbing, and to France in 1824. They made good traveling companions, since they also enjoyed stopping to visit other scientists along the way.

John's first major publication in astronomy came out in 1824. It was a catalog of double, or binary, stars. It earned him the Gold Medal from the Royal Astronomical Society and the Lalande Prize of the Paris Academy. Charles nominated him for the Royal Society presidency in 1831, but John was defeated. This may have been because he, like Charles, was seen as being too "modern," wanting to improve how science was taught. However, 1831 wasn't without its honors, since John was knighted that year.

He followed two loves in the 1830s: studying the structure of comets, particularly Halley's comet, and learning about a new photography technique called the daguerreotype. John actually took some of the earliest English daguerreotypes, including one of his father's astronomical observatory, and might have gone on to be the inventor of modern photography. But, like Charles, he was interested in too many subjects to concentrate on only one. However, John did coin the words photography, negative (of a photograph), and snapshot.

John had a happy home life with his wife and children. Unlike Charles, most of John's children survived: He had nine daughters and three sons. One son, Alexander, also became an astronomer, making it three generations of Herschel astronomers.

In 1935, astronomers honored the Herschels by naming a moon crater J. Herschel and a Mars crater Herschel.

This model of Charles's Analytical Engine shows what may have been the first working computer. Even though he never finished it, as with the Difference Engine, he left all the necessary information. And the Analytical Engine does work.

4

The Analytical Engine

One of Charles's main interests, partly because of the trouble he'd had in Cambridge of finding knowledgeable teachers, was advancing the sciences. In 1830, he published a book called *Reflections on the Decline of Science in England*. In it, he writes, "It cannot have escaped the attention of those . . . who have had opportunities of examining the state of science in other countries, that in England, particularly with respect to the more difficult and abstract sciences, we are much below other nations, not merely of equal rank, but below several even of inferior power."[1]

This book shook up a great many people, particularly those who hadn't realized till then just how badly science was being taught in England. As a result of the book, one year later, the British Association for the Advancement of Science was formed, and Charles must have been quite satisfied to see it. He also was behind the establishment of the Statistical Society of London, now called the Royal Statistical Society.

However, he wasn't too happy about what was happening with his invention. In 1834, he stopped all work on the difference engine. There were two reasons. The first was that the English government was debating, as it continued to do until 1842, on whether or not to keep funding the difference engine. Charles couldn't continue funding it out of his own pocket. He must have been furious at the government's lack of interest in his project, but there was nothing he could do about it.

The second reason was that Charles was already hard at work at designing a bigger and better machine, which he called the analytical engine. This, more so than the difference engine, would be the ancestor of the modern computer.

Actually, Charles had been plotting the analytical engine for some time, giving it so much attention that even though he remained Lucasian Professor of Mathematics at Cambridge for twelve years, he never actually taught a class. By 1834, he had already finished the first drawings of the analytical engine. It would have five parts: the store, the mill, the control, the input, and the output. The store would hold data, the mill would act like the CPU (central processing unit) of a modern computer, the control would run on punched cards that held the program for each job, the input would be for the information request of the user, and the output would print out the answer on punched cards. The analytical engine would be powered by the main source of usable energy in the early nineteenth century, steam. Electricity wasn't yet available.

Some of Charles's fellow scientists insisted that there was nothing new in his work. There already were calculating machines. Charles answered that yes, there were some. But they were very slow and had to be operated completely by hand. Mistakes were common. Time was wasted. His analytical machine would speed up everything and would eliminate most mistakes. It would use what would now be called a computer programming language to analyze information. Like a modern computer, it would provide a link between such things as numbers and the needs of the machine's user. Charles added that his machine's programming would be designed to make quick conclusions. If it "knew" that the next number it was to add was a nine or that a mathematical sequence would be complete with a ten, it would carry out the sequence without needing anyone to add in the numbers by hand.

However, he did need funding. After the trouble he had just had in getting money from the government, he decided that this time around, right or wrong, he wouldn't ask for government help.

It may have been the wrong decision for someone who also wasn't good at fund-raising. Even though he worked on the analytical engine until the day he died in 1871, the project was never finished. He never finished the difference engine, either, nor the "Difference Engine No. 2," which he designed between 1847 and 1849. It wasn't that his ideas were too advanced for his time. Two Swedish scientists, Georg and Edward Scheutz, actually did build a small difference engine in 1834, based on Charles's design, and continued to build other types from 1855 on. It seems a sad irony that in 1859, they even sold one to the English government.

This picture shows punch cards being used by the Jacquard loom. The punches in the cards don't go all the way through, but indent the surface. They look like the Braille system of raised symbols used by blind people to let them read.

The biggest problem with Charles's designs seems to have been Charles himself. Apparently he was one of those people who can never decide when a job is finished. Instead, as soon as he finished a drawing and sent it off to be built, Charles would think of a better way to do the job, then have the work stopped until he could finish the new design. This got in the way of his ever finishing anything.

That problem didn't stop him from dreaming. Clearly predicting the modern computer age, Charles wrote, "The whole of the developments and operations of analysis are now capable of being executed by machinery. . . . As soon as an Analytical Engine exists, it will necessarily guide the future course of science."[2]

This is Georg and Edward Scheutz's difference engine. Charles was angry when he saw someone else "steal" his idea. These rivals built a working difference engine. But it wasn't as good as Charles's design.

One of Babbage's closest and most unlikely friends and colleagues was Augusta Ada King, Countess of Lovelace. What made this friendship so unusual was the fact that Ada, as Charles called her, was so much younger than Charles—she was born in 1815, a year after he graduated Cambridge. Their friendship wasn't romantic, but scientific. Ada was a highly talented mathematician.

Her renown was unusual for a young woman of that era. In the early nineteenth century, women were discouraged from becoming scientists. Such roles weren't supposed to be proper or even possible for women. In fact, some people thought that women's brains couldn't deal with anything as complex as science; others thought that higher learning might somehow harm them.

Ada didn't care what people thought. She was a countess, after all, the daughter of famous poet Lord Byron, and an independent, intelligent woman who did what she wanted. In 1833 she attended Babbage's series of lectures on the difference engine, and she asked to meet him.

The two hit it off and quickly became good friends and colleagues. When they weren't actually working together, Ada and Charles were constantly writing scientific letters back and forth. And it wasn't all work. Ada often teased her friend with sentences like, "The nightingales say you must write to them, but as you can't sing & hate music, I wonder how you will manage to send them any intelligible song!"[3] Charles seems to have put up with Ada's jokes and teasing, even though he hated being teased by anyone else.

Ada was very excited about the difference engine and the analytical engine, and she encouraged Charles to keep working. She even helped by providing suggestions about the new machine he was planning to design. She created her own method for how a machine might automatically repeat steps to solve complicated equations. Because of this work, Ada is now credited as being the first computer programmer. In 1979, a computer programming language was named ADA in her honor.

Unfortunately, Charles's machinery was very expensive. He and Ada raised money by designing game machines, early versions of computers that could play chess or tic-tac-toe. They even tried to work out a mathematical system for betting on sure winners at horse races—but lost a great deal of money when the horses refused to run according to their system.

Sadly, Ada died of cancer when she was only thirty-seven.

Ada, Countess of Lovelace, was an amazing woman. In a time when women weren't supposed to think too much, she was a top mathematician. But she was also the daughter of poet Lord Byron and, as the picture shows, a bit of a flirtatious lady as well.

5

A Bitter End

As Charles grew older, he seems to have lost his cheerful disposition—but he never stopped thinking. In addition to his work on the ancestors of the modern computer, he solved problems in many fields. Some of his other inventions include better lights for lighthouses, uniform postage rates for all of England, and the cowcatcher, the slanted metal piece on the front of steam locomotives used to sweep obstacles off the tracks.[1]

Though he wasn't a music or dance fan, Charles was interested in the lighting effects needed in a ballet. He choreographed a ballet, *Alethes and Iris*, that used an intricate display of colored lights—but it was viewed as being too dangerous, with all those lights posing too great a risk of fire, to ever be performed.[2]

Charles was also interested in codes and code breaking and even locks and lock picking. He wrote about English economics and how they could be improved. One of the only things he tried that wasn't a success for him was politics. Charles was too poor a public speaker and too impatient to make a good politician.

Charles grew more and more unhappy as he grew older. He stopped enjoying himself. He stopped visiting other scientists. At last he turned into a bitter old man. He badly missed his family and his friends. Ada, Countess of Lovelace, had been a dear friend to him. She died on November 27, 1852. John Herschel died on May 11, 1871. Charles was also disappointed that he had never been able to build a working analytical engine.

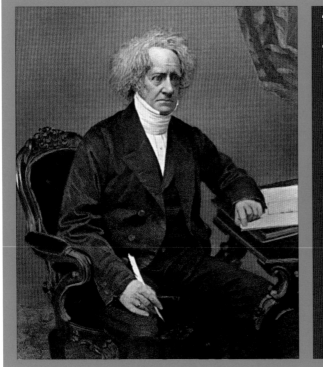

This portrait of John Herschel shows us a man who is quite different from the elegant figure on page 8. He is older, and portrayed this time as a scientist, pen in hand. He also looks rather grim, although the artist may have just meant him to look thoughtful.

He stopped writing and experimenting. People seemed to forget about him. When he died in London on October 18, 1871, few people noticed. There wasn't even an obituary from the Royal Society. It was a sad ending to what had been a very busy life.

Today, however, Charles Babbage is definitely remembered. Scientists argue about why he never finished even one of his machines. Part of the problem probably was his need to keep tinkering with machinery to the point of never finishing anything. There was also the obstacle of money: He could never find enough to build one of the engines. Some scientists also claim that the main reason for Charles's failure to build any of his huge engines had to do with the poor technology of his time.

Two different groups of scientists in the twentieth century tested that theory. In the early twentieth century, a team from London's Science Museum used his original drawings to build a difference engine. The finished machine weighed ten tons and was made up of 4,000 parts. It proved to be a very accurate calculator, far more accurate than any modern pocket calculator. Unfortunately, though, for each calculation, the user had to turn a crank hundreds or thousands of times. That might have been good exercise for the user, but it was not the most efficient way to work calculations.

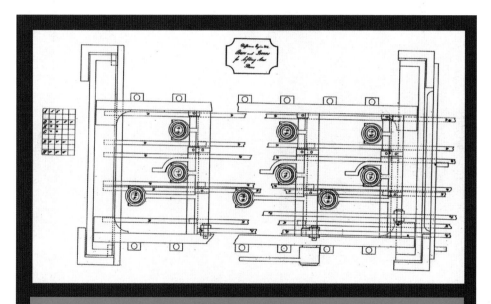

This is one of Charles' many diagrams for the Difference Engine. This one shows a full side view. All the parts are pictured, although measurements aren't on this diagram.

Then, in 1985, a new team from the Science Museum decided to build not the first but the second difference engine. They were careful not to use anything Charles couldn't have used in his day. They showed that even with the technology of Charles's time, he could, indeed, have built a calculating engine—that is, if he'd had the right personality and enough money.

Charles has been remembered in many ways. In 1991, the bicentennial, or two hundredth anniversary, of his birth, the Royal Mail Mint issued a commemorative Charles Babbage postal stamp. A crater at the Moon's north pole is named Crater Babbage in Charles's honor. The Charles Babbage Institute, part of the University of Minnesota, was

In 1985, a team from the London Science Museum built a working model of Charles's second Difference Engine. It can be seen at the London Science Museum. The exhibit also includes information about Charles and the machine.

This is the 1991 English stamp in honor of Charles Babbage. He is pictured as a man with a head full of numbers, which was true enough! He is also honored on the stamp as the father of the computer.

created to preserve and study the history of information technology and processing and their impact on society. The Charles Babbage Foundation was founded in 1977. It helps organizations dedicated to the preservation, interpretation, and dissemination of the history of information technology.

Charles Babbage was one of the rare modern scientists to link scientific ideas to practical use. He was bothered by those scientists who shut themselves off from the outside world, and angry at those businesses that refused to look at new discoveries.

Maybe his biggest problem was that he was a perfectionist. He wouldn't go ahead with something until even the smallest detail was perfect. The constant revising of his work is one of the main reasons he never finished anything. This includes his wanting to write a novel, which he began but never completed.

However, he did succeed at something. In the world of computing and the Internet, Charles Babbage is now generally accepted for what he truly was: the father of modern computing.

The Great
Music War

During most of his life, Charles Babbage liked almost everyone and believed in people's good nature. He even fell for a few scams that were pulled by people pretending to be down on their luck. But toward the end of his life, as he grew bitter about his losses, he grew more and more easily annoyed.

The one thing that he truly hated was street music of any kind, most particularly organ grinders. Unlike his friend John Herschel, who had grown up in a music-loving family, Charles had never appreciated music. He could tolerate classical music in a proper concert hall and could even sit through an opera (although he was far more interested in the stage machinery and how it worked than in the opera itself). Street music, on the other hand, to him was just noise. And as he got older, his hatred of it became an obsession. Street musicians put him into a genuine rage. So did those people who actually enjoyed street musicians, whom Charles described as "those whose minds are entirely unoccupied."[3]

The Great Music War began with an attack by Charles. He seemed unable to ignore the street musicians while he was working, and he claimed he'd lost about twenty-five percent of his valuable work time because of the noise from what he called "those street nuisances."[4] After many letters to the London Times, Charles finally won the first round. What came to be called Babbage's Act banned all street performers in London.

The public was outraged by Babbage's Act. Was this aging mathematician going to deny them their free entertainment? The Great Music War was on in earnest. Street musicians followed Charles whenever he went out, and they played under his windows. Anti-Babbage posters went up in store windows. Children yelled insults at him. One time a brass band played in front of his house for five hours.

Charles refused to give up.

The war over street music lasted throughout the rest of Charles's life. In the end, the street musicians won. Charles, worn out, died. With his death, Babbage's Act was repealed.

Chronology

1791	Born December 26
1810	Attends Trinity College, Cambridge
1814	Graduates from Cambridge; marries Georgiana Whitmore
1815	Moves to London
1816	Becomes a member of the Royal Society
1820	Founds the Analytical Society; cofounds the Royal Astronomical Society and serves as its secretary for four years
1823	Begins building the difference engine
1827	Publishes a table of logarithms calculated with the aid of machinery; father dies; son Charles dies; Georgiana dies
1828	Is named to the Lucasian Professor of Mathematics at Cambridge
1831	Founds the British Association for the Advancement of Science
1832	Publishes *On the Economy of Machinery and Manufactures*
1833	Meets Augusta Ada, Countess of Lovelace, who becomes his friend and colleague; begins work on the analytical engine
1834	Founds the Statistical Society of London
1852	Ada, Countess of Lovelace, dies
1864	Publishes *Passages from the Life of a Philosopher*
1871	John Herschel dies May 11; Charles Babbage dies October 18

Timeline of Discovery

1617   Scottish scientist John Napier invents a calculating device known as Napier's Bones, since the parts were often made from bone.

1623   German scientist Wilhelm Schickard builds a clockwork machine that performs addition, subtraction, multiplication, and division.

1642–1645   French scientist Blaise Pascal invents the Pascaline, a device that more efficiently performs addition and subtraction.

1666   German scientist Gottfried Wilhelm Leibniz writes *De Arte Combinatorica*, in which he predicts computers and calculating devices.

1673   Leibniz designs the Leibniz wheel, a more efficient piece of clockwork machinery that allows more accurate versions of Pascal's device to be built.

1709   Italian scientist Giovanni Poleni invents a more efficient calculating machine.

1728   French engineer M. Falcon invents a loom that can be operated by perforated cards.

1801   French inventor Joseph-Marie Jacquard invents an automated loom, the first working machine that operates from punched cards.

1854   English mathematician George Boole creates Boolean algebra, a specific type of algebra used in modern computers.

1868   American Christopher L. Sholes patents the first practical typewriter.

1878   American James Ritty invents the first cash register.

1885   American bank clerk William Burroughs invents the first successful mechanical adding machine.

1893   German inventor Otto Steiger devises a more efficient calculator for scientific measurements.

1924   IBM is formed.

1937   English scientist Alan M. Turing proves through mathematics that a true computer is possible.

1941–1944   World War II spurs the development of room-sized computers like the Colossus II.

1946   ENIAC, the first large electronic computer, is patented.

1950   Fifty computers exist, each one separately designed and constructed.

1965   There are over eighty computer-manufacturing companies, but computers remain very large and very expensive.

1970   Intel invents the first computer chip.

1975   A New Mexico company, MIT Inc., releases the Altair 8800, the first personal computer; Bill Gates and Paul Allen create Microsoft.

1976   Steve Jobs and Steve Wozniak create Apple Computer.

1977–1990   Hundreds of small computer and software companies are created, although most fail.

1990–present   Personal computers are owned by millions of people around the world, and the Internet connects them.

2005   A group of Hewlett-Packard researchers create a molecular-scale alternative to the transistor.

Chapter Notes

Chapter 1   An Idea Is Born
1. The Science Museum, *Babbage*, "The Tables Crisis,"
www.sciencemuseum.org.uk/on-line/Babbage/page1.asp.
2. Charles Babbage, *Passages from the Life of a Philosopher* (London:
Longman and Green, 1864), p. 31.

Chapter 2   A Mathematician's Boyhood
1. Charles Babbage, *Passages from the Life of a Philosopher* (London:
Longman and Green, 1864), p. 6.
2. Ibid., p. 8–9.
3. Ibid., p. 13.
4. Maboth Moseley, *Irascible Genius: A Life of Charles Babbage,
Inventor* (London: Hutchinson & Co, Ltd., 1964), p. 15.
5. Babbage, p. 31.

Chapter 3   The Difference Engine
1. Charles Babbage, *Passages from the Life of a Philosopher* (London:
Longman and Green, 1864), p. 90.
2. H.W. Buxton, *Memoir of the Life and Labours of the Late Charles
Babbage, Esq. F.R.S.* (Cambridge, MA: The MIT Press, 1988), p. 363.
3. Charles Babbage, *Passages from the Life of a Philosopher* (London:
Longman and Green, 1864), p. 145.
4. Buxton, p. 93.
5. Babbage, p. 49.
6. Buxton, p. 97.

Chapter 4   The Analytical Machine
1. Charles Babbage, *Reflections on the Decline of Science in England*
(London: B. Fellows, 1830), p. 1–2.
2. Charles Babbage, *Passages from the Life of a Philosopher* (London:
Longman and Green, 1864), p. 103.

Chapter 5   A Bitter End
1. Anthony Hyman, *Charles Babbage: Pioneer of the Computer*
(Princeton, NJ: Princeton University Press, 1982), p. 143–44.
2. Ivor Guest, "Babbage's Ballet," *Ballet Magazine*, 1977,
http://www.ballet.co.uk/old/history_js_babbages_ballet.htm

Glossary

algebra
(al-JAH-brah)—a form of advanced mathematics that solves problems using numbers and letters.

analytical engine
(an-ah-LIH-tih-kahl en-JIHN))—an ancestor of the modern computer, designed by Charles Babbage.

astronomer
(ah-STRAH-neh-mer)—someone who studies the stars and planets scientifically.

calculation
(kal-KYOU-lay-shun)—an answer to a mathematical problem.

calculus
(kal-KYOU-lus)—a form of advanced mathematics that depends on calculations.

computer
(kum-PEW-ter)—in the nineteenth century, a human who made mathematical calculations; in the twentieth century, an electronic information storage, retrieval, and processing device.

difference engine
(dif-FER-ense)—an automated form of calculator, designed by Charles Babbage.

Jacquard loom
(jah-KARD loom)—a mechanical loom that wove fabric by punched card instructions.

mathematician
(math-MEH-tih-shun)—someone who studies mathematics, usually professionally.

punched card
(PUNCHT-kard)—a card with holes punched in it in a pattern to make instructions that a machine can "read."

46

For Further Reading

For Young Adults

Champion, Neil. *Charles Babbage*. Chicago: Heinemann Library, 2000.

Collier, Bruce. *Charles Babbage and the Engines of Perfection*. Oxford and New York: Oxford University Press, 1998.

Halacy, Daniel. *Charles Babbage: Father of the Computer*. New York: Crowell-Collier, 1970.

Works Consulted

Agar, Jon. *Turing and the Universal Machine*. Cambridge: Icon Books, 2001.

Aspray, William, ed. *Computing Before Computers*. Ames, IA: Iowa State University Press, 1990.

Babbage, Charles. *Passages from the Life of a Philosopher*. London: Longman, Green, 1864.

———. *Reflections on the Decline of Science in England*. London: B. Fellows, 1830.

Belzer, Jack, Albert G. Holzman, and Allen Kent. *Encyclopedia of Computer Science and Technology*, Vol. 2. New York: Marcel Dekker, Inc., 1975.

Buxton, H. W. *Memoir of the Life and Labours of the Late Charles Babbage, Esq. F.R.S.* Cambridge, MA: The MIT Press, 1988.

Campbell-Kelly, Martin, and William Aspray. *Computer: A History of the Information Machine*. New York: Basic Books, 1996.

Franksen, Ole Immanuel. *Mr. Babbage's Secret: The Tale of a Cypher*. Englewood Cliffs, NJ: Prentice-Hall, 1985.

Goldstine, Herman H. *The Computer: From Pascal to von Neumann*. Princeton, NJ: Princeton University Press, 1972.

Guest, Ivor, "Babbage's Ballet," *Ballet Magazine*, 1977, http://www.ballet.co.uk/old/history_js_babbages_ballet.htm

Hyman, Anthony. *Charles Babbage: Pioneer of the Computer*. Princeton, NJ: Princeton University Press, 1982.

———, ed. *Science and Reform: Selected Works of Charles Babbage*. Cambridge and New York: Cambridge University Press, 1989.

Lee, J.A.N. *Computer Pioneers*. Los Alamitos, CA: IEEE Computer Society Press, 1995.

Magill, Frank N., ed. *The Great Scientists*, Vol. 1. Danbury, CT: Grolier Publishing, 1989.

Morrison, Philip and Emily, eds. *Charles Babbage and His Calculating Engines: Selected Writings by Charles Babbage and Others*. Minneola, NY: Dover Press, 1961.

Moseley, Maboth. *Irascible Genius: A Life of Charles Babbage, Inventor*. London: Hutchinson, 1964.

Saari, Peggy, and Stephen Allison, eds. *Scientists: The Lives and Work of 150 Scientists*. New York: UXL Press, 1996.

Spencer, Douglas D. *The Timetable of Computers*. Ormond Beach, FL: Camelot Publishing Company, 1999.

Swade, Doron. *The Cogwheel Brain*. New York: Little, Brown, 2000.

On the Internet

The MacTutor History of Mathematics Archive, *Charles Babbage* http://www-gap.dcs.st-and.ac.uk/~history/Mathematicians/Babbage.html

The Napoleonic Guide http://www.napoleonguide.com/

The Science Museum, *Babbage* http://www.sciencemuseum.org.uk/on-line/babbage/index.asp

University of Exeter, *The Babbage Pages* http://www.ex.ac.uk/BABBAGE/

The Virtual Museum of Computing, *Charles Babbage, 1791–1871* http://vmoc.museophile.org/babbage/

Index

Abacus 11

Ada, Countess of Lovelace 35, 36, 38

Alethes and Iris, ballet 37

Algebra 15, 16

Babbage, Benjamin 13, 20

    Death 27

Babbage, Charles

    Attends Cambridge school 16

    Attends Devonshire
        school 14–15

    Attends Enfield school 15–16

    Attends Totnes Grammar
        School 16

    Attends Trinity College,
        Cambridge 12, 17–18

    Birth 14

    Birth of son Benjamin
        Herschel 23

    Birth of second son,
        Charles 24

    Childhood in London 14

    Death of Charles (son) 27

    Death of Georgiana 27

    Designs first Analytical
        Engine 30, 32–33

    Designs first Difference
        Engine 22, 25–27, 28,
        31–32, 39

    Dies 38

    Elected member, Royal
        Society 24

    Elected Lucasian Professor
        of Mathematics 28, 32

    Founds Royal Astronomical
        Society 25, 26

    Marries Georgiana
        Witmore 20

    Meets Georgiana
        Witmore 18

    Publishes a table of
        logarithms 27

    Publishes *Reflections on the
        Decline of Science* 31

    Sets up Analytical Society 19

    Studies Mount Vesuvius 28

    Tries to summon devil 15

Babbage, Elizabeth "Betsy" 13

British Association for the
    Advancement of Science 31

Buxton, H. Wilmot 24

Charles Babbage Foundation 41

Charles Babbage Institute 40

Charles Babbage postal
    stamp 40, 41

Crater Babbage 40

Difference Engine No. 2 33

Duke of Ellington 21, 28

Great Music War 42

Herschel, John 7, 8, 23, 25, 27, 29, 38

    Death 38

Jacquard loom 9, 10

Lacroix, Sylvestre 19

London's Science Museum 39, 40

Napoleonic Wars 21

Peacock, George 19

Punched cards 32, 33

Royal Mail Mint 40

Royal Society 7, 24, 25, 26, 28, 38

Royal Statistical Society 31

Scheutz, Georg and Edward 33, 34

Witmore, Georgiana 18, 19, 20, 23, 24